50 Quick and Easy Recipes for Home

By: Kelly Johnson

Table of Contents

- Spaghetti Aglio e Olio
- Caprese Salad
- Grilled Cheese Sandwich
- Avocado Toast
- Greek Salad
- Margherita Pizza
- Pesto Pasta
- BLT Sandwich
- Vegetable Stir-Fry
- Tomato Basil Soup
- Tuna Salad Sandwich
- Chicken Caesar Salad
- Quesadillas
- Egg Salad Sandwich
- Veggie Wrap
- Hummus and Veggie Platter
- Cheese Quesadillas
- Tomato and Mozzarella Panini
- Caesar Salad Wrap
- Baked Potato with Sour Cream and Chives
- Chicken Wrap
- Nachos with Cheese and Salsa
- Greek Yogurt Parfait with Fruit and Granola
- Shrimp Tacos
- Veggie Omelette
- Turkey and Cheese Roll-Ups
- Spinach and Feta Stuffed Chicken Breast
- Black Bean Quesadillas
- Tuna Melt Sandwich
- Margherita Flatbread
- Chicken Fajitas
- Pasta Primavera
- Cobb Salad
- Chicken Burrito Bowl
- Ratatouille

- Egg and Avocado Breakfast Wrap
- Buffalo Chicken Wraps
- Quinoa Salad with Veggies
- Grilled Chicken Caesar Wrap
- Turkey Chili
- Veggie Stir-Fry with Tofu
- Chicken and Rice Soup
- Beef Tacos
- Avocado and Tomato Grilled Cheese
- Greek Yogurt Chicken Salad
- Lentil Soup
- Beef Stir-Fry with Broccoli
- Spinach and Mushroom Quesadillas
- Shrimp Stir-Fry with Rice
- Caprese Panini

Spaghetti Aglio e Olio

Ingredients:

- 8 ounces (225g) spaghetti
- 4 cloves garlic, thinly sliced
- 1/4 cup extra virgin olive oil
- 1/2 teaspoon red pepper flakes (adjust to taste)
- Salt, to taste
- Freshly ground black pepper, to taste
- Fresh parsley, chopped (for garnish)
- Grated Parmesan cheese (optional, for serving)

Instructions:

1. Cook the spaghetti according to the package instructions in a large pot of salted boiling water until al dente. Reserve about 1/2 cup of pasta cooking water, then drain the spaghetti and set aside.
2. While the spaghetti is cooking, heat the olive oil in a large skillet over medium heat. Add the sliced garlic and red pepper flakes to the skillet.
3. Cook the garlic, stirring frequently, until it turns golden and fragrant, but be careful not to let it burn. This should take about 1-2 minutes.
4. Add the cooked spaghetti to the skillet with the garlic and red pepper flakes. Toss well to coat the spaghetti evenly with the garlic-infused olive oil.
5. If the spaghetti seems too dry, add a splash of the reserved pasta cooking water to loosen it up and create a light sauce. Season with salt and black pepper to taste.
6. Transfer the spaghetti aglio e olio to serving plates or a large serving platter.
7. Garnish with freshly chopped parsley for color and freshness.
8. Serve the spaghetti aglio e olio hot, with grated Parmesan cheese on the side for sprinkling, if desired.
9. Enjoy this simple yet flavorful pasta dish as a quick and satisfying meal!

Caprese Salad

Ingredients:

- 3-4 ripe tomatoes, sliced
- 8 ounces (225g) fresh mozzarella cheese, sliced
- Fresh basil leaves
- Extra virgin olive oil
- Balsamic vinegar
- Salt, to taste
- Freshly ground black pepper, to taste

Instructions:

1. Arrange the tomato slices on a serving platter or individual plates, alternating with slices of fresh mozzarella cheese.
2. Tuck fresh basil leaves in between the tomato and mozzarella slices.
3. Drizzle extra virgin olive oil over the tomatoes and mozzarella. Use a good quality olive oil for the best flavor.
4. Drizzle balsamic vinegar over the salad. You can use regular balsamic vinegar or balsamic glaze for a thicker consistency and sweeter flavor.
5. Season the salad with salt and freshly ground black pepper to taste.
6. Serve the Caprese salad immediately as a refreshing appetizer or side dish.
7. Enjoy the vibrant colors and delicious flavors of this classic Italian salad!

Note: You can also make individual Caprese salad skewers by threading cherry tomatoes, small mozzarella balls (bocconcini), and basil leaves onto toothpicks or skewers. Drizzle with olive oil and balsamic vinegar before serving.

Grilled Cheese Sandwich

Ingredients:

- 2 slices of bread (white, whole wheat, or your choice)
- 2-3 slices of cheese (Cheddar, American, Swiss, or your favorite melting cheese)
- Butter or margarine, softened

Instructions:

1. Heat a skillet or griddle over medium-low heat.
2. Spread butter or margarine on one side of each slice of bread.
3. Place one slice of bread, buttered side down, on the heated skillet or griddle.
4. Layer the cheese slices evenly on top of the bread slice.
5. Place the second slice of bread on top, buttered side facing up.
6. Cook the sandwich for 2-3 minutes on each side, or until the bread is golden brown and the cheese is melted.
7. If desired, you can press down on the sandwich with a spatula while cooking to help flatten it and ensure even melting of the cheese.
8. Once both sides are golden brown and the cheese is melted, remove the sandwich from the skillet or griddle.
9. Let the grilled cheese sandwich cool for a minute or two before serving.
10. Slice the sandwich in half diagonally or into quarters, if desired.
11. Serve the grilled cheese sandwich hot with your favorite dipping sauce, soup, or enjoy it on its own.
12. Feel free to customize your grilled cheese sandwich by adding other ingredients like sliced tomatoes, cooked bacon, avocado, or caramelized onions for extra flavor.

Avocado Toast

Ingredients:

- 1 ripe avocado
- 2 slices of bread (whole grain, sourdough, or your choice)
- Salt, to taste
- Black pepper, to taste
- Red pepper flakes (optional)
- Lemon juice (optional)
- Optional toppings: sliced tomatoes, poached or fried eggs, feta cheese, arugula, smoked salmon, etc.

Instructions:

1. Cut the avocado in half lengthwise and remove the pit. Scoop out the flesh into a bowl.
2. Use a fork to mash the avocado until smooth or slightly chunky, depending on your preference.
3. Season the mashed avocado with salt, black pepper, and red pepper flakes to taste. Add a squeeze of lemon juice if desired for extra flavor and to prevent browning.
4. Toast the slices of bread until golden brown and crispy.
5. Spread the mashed avocado evenly onto the toasted bread slices.
6. Top the avocado toast with your desired toppings, such as sliced tomatoes, poached or fried eggs, crumbled feta cheese, arugula, or smoked salmon.
7. Sprinkle with additional salt, black pepper, or red pepper flakes if desired.
8. Serve the avocado toast immediately while the bread is still warm and crispy.
9. Enjoy this nutritious and flavorful avocado toast for breakfast, brunch, or as a satisfying snack any time of day!

Greek Salad

Ingredients:

- 2 large tomatoes, chopped
- 1 cucumber, chopped
- 1 red onion, thinly sliced
- 1 green bell pepper, chopped
- 1/2 cup Kalamata olives, pitted
- 4 ounces (about 1 cup) feta cheese, crumbled
- 1/4 cup extra virgin olive oil
- 2 tablespoons red wine vinegar
- 1 teaspoon dried oregano
- Salt and black pepper, to taste
- Fresh parsley or basil, chopped (for garnish)

Instructions:

1. In a large mixing bowl, combine the chopped tomatoes, cucumber, red onion, green bell pepper, and Kalamata olives.
2. Add the crumbled feta cheese to the bowl.
3. In a small bowl or jar, whisk together the extra virgin olive oil, red wine vinegar, dried oregano, salt, and black pepper to make the dressing.
4. Pour the dressing over the salad ingredients in the large mixing bowl.
5. Toss the salad gently to coat all the vegetables and feta cheese evenly with the dressing.
6. Taste the salad and adjust the seasoning if needed, adding more salt, pepper, or vinegar to taste.
7. Transfer the Greek salad to a serving platter or individual plates.
8. Garnish the salad with chopped fresh parsley or basil for a pop of color and freshness.
9. Serve the Greek salad immediately as a refreshing appetizer or side dish.
10. Enjoy the vibrant flavors and textures of this classic Greek salad!

Margherita Pizza

Ingredients:

- 1 ball of pizza dough (homemade or store-bought)
- 1/2 cup marinara sauce or pizza sauce
- 8 ounces fresh mozzarella cheese, sliced
- Fresh basil leaves
- Extra virgin olive oil, for drizzling
- Salt and black pepper, to taste
- Cornmeal or flour, for dusting (if using homemade dough)

Instructions:

1. Preheat your oven to the highest temperature possible, typically around 500°F (260°C) or higher. If you have a pizza stone, place it in the oven to preheat as well.
2. Roll out the pizza dough on a lightly floured surface to your desired thickness. If using homemade dough, you can also sprinkle some cornmeal on the pizza peel to prevent sticking.
3. Transfer the rolled-out dough to a pizza peel or baking sheet lined with parchment paper.
4. Spread the marinara sauce evenly over the pizza dough, leaving a small border around the edges.
5. Arrange the slices of fresh mozzarella cheese on top of the sauce.
6. Tear the fresh basil leaves and scatter them over the cheese.
7. Season the pizza with a pinch of salt and black pepper, to taste.
8. Drizzle a little extra virgin olive oil over the pizza.
9. Carefully transfer the pizza to the preheated oven, either by sliding it onto the pizza stone (if using) or placing the baking sheet directly in the oven.
10. Bake the pizza for 10-12 minutes, or until the crust is golden brown and the cheese is melted and bubbly.
11. Once the pizza is done, remove it from the oven and let it cool slightly.
12. Slice the Margherita pizza into wedges and serve hot.
13. Enjoy the classic flavors of tomato, mozzarella, and basil in this delicious Margherita pizza!

Pesto Pasta

Ingredients:

- 8 ounces (225g) pasta of your choice (spaghetti, penne, fusilli, etc.)
- 2 cups fresh basil leaves, packed
- 1/2 cup grated Parmesan cheese
- 1/2 cup pine nuts or walnuts
- 2 cloves garlic, peeled
- 1/2 cup extra virgin olive oil
- Salt and black pepper, to taste
- Optional toppings: cherry tomatoes, grilled chicken, cooked shrimp, roasted vegetables, etc.

Instructions:

1. Cook the pasta according to the package instructions in a large pot of salted boiling water until al dente. Reserve about 1/2 cup of pasta cooking water, then drain the pasta and set aside.
2. While the pasta is cooking, make the pesto sauce. In a food processor or blender, combine the fresh basil leaves, grated Parmesan cheese, pine nuts or walnuts, and garlic cloves.
3. Pulse the ingredients until finely chopped.
4. With the food processor or blender running, gradually pour in the extra virgin olive oil until the mixture becomes smooth and well combined. You may need to stop and scrape down the sides of the bowl occasionally.
5. Season the pesto sauce with salt and black pepper to taste. Adjust the seasoning if needed.
6. In a large mixing bowl, toss the cooked pasta with the pesto sauce until well coated. If the pasta seems too dry, you can add a splash of the reserved pasta cooking water to loosen it up.
7. Serve the pesto pasta hot, topped with your choice of optional toppings, such as cherry tomatoes, grilled chicken, cooked shrimp, or roasted vegetables.
8. Enjoy the vibrant flavors of this delicious pesto pasta as a quick and satisfying meal!

BLT Sandwich

Ingredients:

- 6 slices of bacon
- 4 slices of bread (white, whole wheat, or your choice)
- 2 leaves of lettuce
- 1 large tomato, sliced
- Mayonnaise
- Salt and pepper, to taste

Instructions:

1. Cook the bacon in a skillet over medium heat until crispy. Remove the bacon from the skillet and drain on paper towels.
2. Toast the slices of bread until golden brown.
3. Spread mayonnaise on one side of each slice of bread.
4. Layer the lettuce leaves on two slices of bread.
5. Place the sliced tomatoes on top of the lettuce.
6. Season the tomatoes with salt and pepper to taste.
7. Place the crispy bacon slices on top of the tomatoes.
8. Top with the remaining slices of bread, mayonnaise side down, to form sandwiches.
9. Cut the sandwiches in half diagonally, if desired.
10. Serve the BLT sandwiches immediately, and enjoy the delicious combination of flavors and textures!

Feel free to customize your BLT sandwich by adding avocado slices, a fried egg, or your favorite cheese for extra flavor.

Vegetable Stir-Fry

Ingredients:

- 2 tablespoons vegetable oil
- 2 cloves garlic, minced
- 1 tablespoon ginger, minced
- 4 cups mixed vegetables (such as bell peppers, broccoli, carrots, snap peas, mushrooms, etc.), sliced or chopped
- 1/4 cup soy sauce
- 2 tablespoons oyster sauce (optional)
- 1 tablespoon sesame oil
- Cooked rice or noodles, for serving
- Sesame seeds and sliced green onions, for garnish (optional)

Instructions:

1. Heat the vegetable oil in a large skillet or wok over medium-high heat.
2. Add the minced garlic and ginger to the skillet, and stir-fry for about 30 seconds, or until fragrant.
3. Add the mixed vegetables to the skillet, and stir-fry for 3-5 minutes, or until they are crisp-tender.
4. In a small bowl, mix together the soy sauce and oyster sauce (if using).
5. Pour the sauce mixture over the vegetables in the skillet, and stir to coat evenly.
6. Drizzle the sesame oil over the vegetables, and toss to combine.
7. Continue to cook for another 1-2 minutes, or until the sauce has thickened slightly and the vegetables are cooked to your liking.
8. Remove the skillet from the heat.
9. Serve the vegetable stir-fry over cooked rice or noodles.
10. Garnish with sesame seeds and sliced green onions, if desired.
11. Enjoy your delicious and nutritious vegetable stir-fry!

Tomato Basil Soup

Ingredients:

- 2 tablespoons olive oil
- 1 onion, chopped
- 2 cloves garlic, minced
- 2 (28-ounce) cans whole tomatoes, with their juices
- 1 cup vegetable broth or chicken broth
- 1/4 cup fresh basil leaves, chopped (plus extra for garnish)
- Salt and pepper, to taste
- 1/2 cup heavy cream or half-and-half (optional)

Instructions:

1. Heat the olive oil in a large pot over medium heat.
2. Add the chopped onion to the pot, and cook for 5-7 minutes, or until softened and translucent.
3. Add the minced garlic to the pot, and cook for an additional 1-2 minutes, or until fragrant.
4. Pour the cans of whole tomatoes (with their juices) into the pot, breaking up the tomatoes with a spoon or spatula.
5. Add the vegetable or chicken broth to the pot, and stir to combine.
6. Bring the soup to a simmer, and let it cook for 15-20 minutes, stirring occasionally.
7. Stir in the chopped basil leaves, and season the soup with salt and pepper to taste.
8. If using, stir in the heavy cream or half-and-half to add richness to the soup. You can omit this ingredient if you prefer a dairy-free version.
9. Use an immersion blender to puree the soup until smooth and creamy. Alternatively, you can carefully transfer the soup in batches to a blender and blend until smooth, then return it to the pot.
10. Taste the soup and adjust the seasoning if needed.
11. Serve the tomato basil soup hot, garnished with additional chopped basil leaves.
12. Enjoy your delicious and comforting tomato basil soup!

Tuna Salad Sandwich

Ingredients:

- 1 can (5 ounces) tuna, drained
- 2 tablespoons mayonnaise
- 1 tablespoon plain Greek yogurt (optional, for creaminess)
- 1 tablespoon finely chopped celery
- 1 tablespoon finely chopped red onion
- 1 teaspoon lemon juice
- Salt and pepper, to taste
- 4 slices of bread (white, whole wheat, or your choice)
- Lettuce leaves and tomato slices, for serving (optional)

Instructions:

1. In a mixing bowl, combine the drained tuna, mayonnaise, Greek yogurt (if using), chopped celery, chopped red onion, and lemon juice.
2. Stir the ingredients together until well combined.
3. Season the tuna salad with salt and pepper to taste. Adjust the seasoning if needed.
4. Spread the tuna salad evenly onto two slices of bread.
5. If desired, top the tuna salad with lettuce leaves and tomato slices for added freshness.
6. Place the remaining slices of bread on top to form sandwiches.
7. Cut the sandwiches in half diagonally, if desired.
8. Serve the tuna salad sandwiches immediately, or wrap them in plastic wrap or foil for later.
9. Enjoy your delicious and satisfying tuna salad sandwiches for lunch or a quick meal on the go!

Chicken Caesar Salad

Ingredients:

- 2 boneless, skinless chicken breasts
- Salt and black pepper, to taste
- 1 tablespoon olive oil
- 1 large head of romaine lettuce, chopped
- 1 cup croutons (store-bought or homemade)
- 1/2 cup grated Parmesan cheese
- Caesar dressing (store-bought or homemade)

For the Caesar dressing:

- 1/2 cup mayonnaise
- 2 tablespoons grated Parmesan cheese
- 1 tablespoon lemon juice
- 1 teaspoon Dijon mustard
- 1 clove garlic, minced
- Salt and black pepper, to taste

Instructions:

1. Season the chicken breasts with salt and black pepper on both sides.
2. Heat the olive oil in a skillet or grill pan over medium-high heat. Add the chicken breasts to the pan and cook for 6-8 minutes per side, or until cooked through and no longer pink in the center. Remove from the heat and let rest for a few minutes before slicing.
3. While the chicken is cooking, prepare the Caesar dressing. In a small bowl, whisk together the mayonnaise, grated Parmesan cheese, lemon juice, Dijon mustard, minced garlic, salt, and black pepper until smooth and well combined. Adjust the seasoning to taste.
4. In a large mixing bowl, toss the chopped romaine lettuce with the Caesar dressing until evenly coated.
5. Divide the dressed romaine lettuce among serving plates or bowls.

6. Top each serving with sliced grilled chicken breast, croutons, and grated Parmesan cheese.
7. Serve the chicken Caesar salad immediately, and enjoy the classic combination of flavors and textures!

Feel free to customize your chicken Caesar salad by adding additional toppings such as cherry tomatoes, sliced cucumbers, avocado, or hard-boiled eggs.

Quesadillas

Ingredients:

- 4 large flour tortillas
- 2 cups shredded cheese (such as cheddar, Monterey Jack, or a Mexican blend)
- Optional fillings: cooked chicken, cooked steak, sautéed vegetables, black beans, corn, diced tomatoes, jalapeños, etc.
- Cooking oil or butter, for frying
- Optional toppings: sour cream, salsa, guacamole, chopped cilantro, diced onions, etc.

Instructions:

1. Place a large skillet or frying pan over medium heat.
2. Place one tortilla on a flat surface. Sprinkle half of the shredded cheese evenly over one half of the tortilla.
3. Add any desired fillings, such as cooked chicken, sautéed vegetables, beans, etc., over the cheese.
4. Sprinkle the remaining shredded cheese over the fillings.
5. Fold the empty half of the tortilla over the cheese and fillings to create a half-moon shape.
6. Repeat the process with the remaining tortillas and fillings.
7. Lightly brush the skillet with cooking oil or melt butter over medium heat.
8. Carefully transfer one quesadilla to the skillet and cook for 2-3 minutes, or until the bottom is golden brown and crispy.
9. Carefully flip the quesadilla using a spatula and cook for an additional 2-3 minutes on the other side, until the cheese is melted and the tortilla is golden brown and crispy.
10. Remove the cooked quesadilla from the skillet and place it on a cutting board. Allow it to cool for a minute before slicing into wedges.
11. Repeat the cooking process with the remaining quesadillas.
12. Serve the quesadillas hot, with optional toppings such as sour cream, salsa, guacamole, chopped cilantro, and diced onions on the side.
13. Enjoy your delicious and cheesy quesadillas as a snack, appetizer, or main dish!

Egg Salad Sandwich

Ingredients:

- 6 hard-boiled eggs, peeled and chopped
- 1/4 cup mayonnaise
- 1 tablespoon Dijon mustard
- 2 tablespoons finely chopped celery
- 2 tablespoons finely chopped red onion
- Salt and black pepper, to taste
- 8 slices of bread (white, whole wheat, or your choice)
- Lettuce leaves and tomato slices, for serving (optional)

Instructions:

1. In a mixing bowl, combine the chopped hard-boiled eggs, mayonnaise, Dijon mustard, chopped celery, and chopped red onion.
2. Stir the ingredients together until well combined.
3. Season the egg salad with salt and black pepper to taste. Adjust the seasoning if needed.
4. Spread the egg salad evenly onto four slices of bread.
5. If desired, top the egg salad with lettuce leaves and tomato slices for added freshness.
6. Place the remaining slices of bread on top to form sandwiches.
7. Cut the sandwiches in half diagonally, if desired.
8. Serve the egg salad sandwiches immediately, or wrap them in plastic wrap or foil for later.
9. Enjoy your delicious and satisfying egg salad sandwiches for lunch or a quick meal on the go!

Veggie Wrap

Ingredients:

- Large whole wheat or spinach tortillas
- Hummus or cream cheese, for spreading
- Assorted fresh vegetables, thinly sliced or shredded (such as lettuce, spinach, bell peppers, cucumbers, carrots, tomatoes, avocado, etc.)
- Optional add-ons: sliced olives, sun-dried tomatoes, sprouts, shredded cheese, etc.
- Optional protein: grilled tofu, chickpeas, black beans, or cooked quinoa

Instructions:

1. Lay out a tortilla on a clean, flat surface.
2. Spread a layer of hummus or cream cheese evenly over the entire surface of the tortilla, leaving a small border around the edges.
3. Arrange your desired vegetables and optional add-ons in the center of the tortilla, leaving some space around the edges to facilitate rolling.
4. If adding protein, place it on top of the vegetables.
5. Fold the sides of the tortilla inward, then roll it up tightly from the bottom, tucking in the fillings as you go.
6. Continue rolling until you reach the end of the tortilla, and press lightly to seal the wrap.
7. Repeat the process with the remaining tortillas and fillings.
8. If serving immediately, slice the wraps in half diagonally or into bite-sized pieces.
9. If saving for later, wrap each veggie wrap tightly in plastic wrap or foil to keep them fresh.
10. Serve the veggie wraps as is, or pair them with your favorite dipping sauce or dressing.
11. Enjoy your delicious and customizable veggie wraps for a quick and healthy meal!

Hummus and Veggie Platter

Ingredients:

- Hummus (store-bought or homemade)
- Assorted fresh vegetables, such as:
    - Carrot sticks
    - Celery sticks
    - Cucumber slices
    - Bell pepper strips (red, yellow, green)
    - Cherry tomatoes
    - Sugar snap peas
    - Radishes
    - Broccoli florets
    - Cauliflower florets
- Olives
- Pita bread or pita chips
- Optional garnishes: fresh herbs (parsley, cilantro), lemon wedges, olive oil, paprika, or sesame seeds

Instructions:

1. Choose a large platter or serving tray to arrange your hummus and veggie spread.
2. Spoon the hummus into a bowl and place it in the center of the platter.
3. Arrange the assorted fresh vegetables around the hummus bowl in an aesthetically pleasing manner, leaving space for the pita bread or chips.
4. You can place the vegetables in individual piles or groups, or spread them out in a decorative pattern.
5. Scatter olives around the platter for added flavor and visual appeal.
6. If using, place a stack of pita bread or pita chips on one side of the platter.
7. Optional: Garnish the hummus with a drizzle of olive oil, a sprinkle of paprika or sesame seeds, and fresh herbs. Arrange lemon wedges around the platter for squeezing over the hummus.
8. Serve the hummus and veggie platter immediately, along with the pita bread or chips for dipping.

9. Enjoy the vibrant colors and flavors of this healthy and delicious appetizer or snack!

Feel free to customize your hummus and veggie platter with your favorite vegetables and additional accompaniments, such as crackers, breadsticks, or cheese.

Cheese Quesadillas

Ingredients:

- 4 large flour tortillas
- 2 cups shredded cheese (such as cheddar, Monterey Jack, or a Mexican blend)
- Cooking oil or butter, for frying (optional)
- Optional add-ons: cooked chicken, cooked steak, sautéed vegetables, black beans, corn, diced tomatoes, jalapeños, etc.
- Optional toppings: sour cream, salsa, guacamole, chopped cilantro, diced onions, etc.

Instructions:

1. Heat a large skillet or frying pan over medium heat.
2. Place one tortilla in the skillet and sprinkle half of the shredded cheese evenly over the entire surface of the tortilla.
3. Add any desired add-ons, such as cooked chicken, sautéed vegetables, beans, etc., over the cheese.
4. Sprinkle the remaining shredded cheese over the add-ons.
5. Place another tortilla on top to form a sandwich.
6. Cook the quesadilla for 2-3 minutes on one side, or until the bottom tortilla is golden brown and crispy, and the cheese is starting to melt.
7. Carefully flip the quesadilla using a spatula and cook for an additional 2-3 minutes on the other side, until the cheese is completely melted and the tortilla is golden brown and crispy.
8. Remove the cooked quesadilla from the skillet and place it on a cutting board. Allow it to cool for a minute before slicing into wedges.
9. Repeat the cooking process with the remaining tortillas and fillings.
10. Serve the cheese quesadillas hot, with optional toppings such as sour cream, salsa, guacamole, chopped cilantro, and diced onions on the side.
11. Enjoy your delicious and cheesy cheese quesadillas as a snack, appetizer, or main dish!

Tomato and Mozzarella Panini

Ingredients:

- 4 slices of bread (such as ciabatta, sourdough, or Italian bread)
- 8 slices of fresh mozzarella cheese
- 2 ripe tomatoes, thinly sliced
- Fresh basil leaves
- Olive oil, for brushing
- Salt and black pepper, to taste
- Optional: balsamic glaze or pesto sauce for extra flavor

Instructions:

1. Preheat a panini press or grill pan over medium heat.
2. Brush one side of each slice of bread lightly with olive oil.
3. On the non-oiled side of two bread slices, layer the mozzarella cheese slices, followed by the tomato slices and fresh basil leaves. Season with salt and black pepper to taste.
4. Optional: Drizzle a small amount of balsamic glaze or spread pesto sauce on top of the basil leaves for extra flavor.
5. Top each sandwich with the remaining two bread slices, oiled side facing up.
6. Place the sandwiches on the preheated panini press or grill pan.
7. If using a panini press, close the lid and cook the sandwiches for 4-5 minutes, or until the bread is golden brown and crispy, and the cheese is melted.
8. If using a grill pan, place a heavy skillet or press on top of the sandwiches to press them down. Cook for 2-3 minutes on each side, or until the bread is golden brown and crispy, and the cheese is melted.
9. Carefully remove the sandwiches from the panini press or grill pan and transfer them to a cutting board.
10. Allow the sandwiches to cool for a minute or two before slicing them in half diagonally.
11. Serve the tomato and mozzarella panini hot, and enjoy the delicious combination of flavors and textures!

Feel free to customize your panini by adding other ingredients like sliced ham, roasted red peppers, or caramelized onions for extra flavor.

Caesar Salad Wrap

Ingredients:

- 1 large flour tortilla or wrap
- 1 cup chopped romaine lettuce
- 1/4 cup Caesar dressing (store-bought or homemade)
- 1/4 cup grated Parmesan cheese
- 1/2 cup croutons, crushed
- Optional add-ons: grilled chicken strips, bacon bits, cherry tomatoes, avocado slices, etc.

Instructions:

1. Lay the flour tortilla or wrap flat on a clean surface.
2. Spread the chopped romaine lettuce evenly over the center of the tortilla, leaving a border around the edges.
3. Drizzle the Caesar dressing over the lettuce.
4. Sprinkle the grated Parmesan cheese over the dressing.
5. Add the crushed croutons on top of the cheese.
6. If using any optional add-ons, such as grilled chicken strips or bacon bits, arrange them over the lettuce mixture.
7. Carefully fold the sides of the tortilla inward, then roll it up tightly from the bottom, tucking in the fillings as you go.
8. Continue rolling until you reach the end of the tortilla, and press lightly to seal the wrap.
9. If serving immediately, slice the wrap in half diagonally or into bite-sized pieces.
10. If saving for later, wrap the Caesar salad wrap tightly in plastic wrap or foil to keep it fresh.
11. Serve the Caesar salad wrap immediately, and enjoy the delicious combination of flavors and textures!

Feel free to customize your Caesar salad wrap with your favorite ingredients and additional toppings to suit your taste preferences.

Baked Potato with Sour Cream and Chives

Ingredients:

- 4 large russet potatoes
- Olive oil
- Salt
- Pepper
- Sour cream
- Fresh chives, chopped

Instructions:

1. Preheat your oven to 400°F (200°C).
2. Scrub the potatoes clean under running water and pat them dry with paper towels.
3. Pierce each potato several times with a fork to allow steam to escape during baking.
4. Rub the potatoes with olive oil, then sprinkle them with salt and pepper.
5. Place the potatoes directly on the oven rack or on a baking sheet lined with parchment paper.
6. Bake the potatoes for 45 minutes to 1 hour, or until they are tender when pierced with a fork.
7. Remove the potatoes from the oven and let them cool for a few minutes.
8. Carefully slice each potato open lengthwise, then fluff the insides with a fork.
9. Top each baked potato with a dollop of sour cream and a sprinkle of chopped fresh chives.
10. Serve the baked potatoes with sour cream and chives immediately as a side dish or light meal.
11. Enjoy the creamy and flavorful combination of sour cream and chives with the fluffy baked potato!

Chicken Wrap

Ingredients:

- 1 large flour tortilla or wrap
- 1 cooked chicken breast, thinly sliced or shredded
- 1/4 cup shredded lettuce or baby spinach leaves
- 1/4 cup diced tomatoes
- 1/4 cup shredded cheese (such as cheddar, Monterey Jack, or a Mexican blend)
- Optional add-ons: sliced avocado, sliced bell peppers, sliced cucumber, sliced red onion, etc.
- Optional sauce: ranch dressing, barbecue sauce, honey mustard, buffalo sauce, tzatziki sauce, etc.

Instructions:

1. Lay the flour tortilla or wrap flat on a clean surface.
2. Place the cooked chicken breast slices or shredded chicken in the center of the tortilla.
3. Add the shredded lettuce or baby spinach leaves on top of the chicken.
4. Sprinkle the diced tomatoes and shredded cheese over the lettuce.
5. If using any optional add-ons, such as sliced avocado or bell peppers, arrange them over the cheese.
6. If desired, drizzle your favorite sauce over the fillings. Some popular options include ranch dressing, barbecue sauce, honey mustard, buffalo sauce, or tzatziki sauce.
7. Carefully fold the sides of the tortilla inward, then roll it up tightly from the bottom, tucking in the fillings as you go.
8. Continue rolling until you reach the end of the tortilla, and press lightly to seal the wrap.
9. If serving immediately, slice the wrap in half diagonally or into bite-sized pieces.
10. If saving for later, wrap the chicken wrap tightly in plastic wrap or foil to keep it fresh.
11. Serve the chicken wrap immediately, and enjoy the delicious combination of flavors and textures!

Feel free to customize your chicken wrap with your favorite ingredients and sauces to suit your taste preferences.

Nachos with Cheese and Salsa

Ingredients:

- Tortilla chips
- 1 cup shredded cheese (such as cheddar, Monterey Jack, or a Mexican blend)
- 1/2 cup salsa (store-bought or homemade)
- Optional toppings: sliced jalapeños, diced tomatoes, sliced black olives, sliced green onions, diced avocado, sour cream, guacamole, etc.

Instructions:

1. Preheat your oven to 375°F (190°C).
2. Spread a single layer of tortilla chips on a large baking sheet.
3. Sprinkle the shredded cheese evenly over the tortilla chips.
4. Add any desired toppings, such as sliced jalapeños, diced tomatoes, sliced black olives, etc., over the cheese.
5. Place the baking sheet in the preheated oven and bake for 5-7 minutes, or until the cheese is melted and bubbly.
6. Remove the nachos from the oven and let them cool slightly.
7. Drizzle the salsa over the melted cheese and toppings.
8. If desired, add additional toppings such as sliced green onions, diced avocado, sour cream, or guacamole on top of the salsa.
9. Serve the nachos with cheese and salsa immediately, and enjoy the delicious combination of flavors and textures!

Note: Feel free to customize your nachos with your favorite toppings and sauces. You can also add cooked ground beef, shredded chicken, or refried beans for extra protein. Just layer them on top of the cheese before baking.

Greek Yogurt Parfait with Fruit and Granola

Ingredients:

- Greek yogurt (plain or flavored)
- Fresh fruit (such as berries, sliced bananas, diced peaches, etc.)
- Granola (store-bought or homemade)
- Optional toppings: honey, maple syrup, agave nectar, chopped nuts, coconut flakes, etc.

Instructions:

1. Start by layering the ingredients in a glass or bowl. Begin with a spoonful of Greek yogurt at the bottom.
2. Add a layer of fresh fruit on top of the yogurt. You can use one type of fruit or a combination of different fruits.
3. Sprinkle a layer of granola over the fruit. The granola adds crunch and texture to the parfait.
4. Repeat the layers as desired, alternating between Greek yogurt, fruit, and granola, until the glass or bowl is filled.
5. Drizzle a small amount of honey, maple syrup, or agave nectar over the top of the parfait for added sweetness, if desired.
6. Optional: Sprinkle chopped nuts or coconut flakes on top for extra flavor and texture.
7. Serve the Greek yogurt parfait immediately, and enjoy the delicious combination of creamy yogurt, sweet fruit, and crunchy granola!

Feel free to customize your Greek yogurt parfait with your favorite fruits, granola flavors, and toppings to suit your taste preferences. You can also make it ahead of time and store it in the refrigerator for a quick and convenient breakfast or snack option.

Shrimp Tacos

Ingredients:

- 1 lb (450g) large shrimp, peeled and deveined
- 2 tablespoons olive oil
- 1 teaspoon chili powder
- 1/2 teaspoon ground cumin
- 1/2 teaspoon paprika
- Salt and pepper, to taste
- 8 small flour or corn tortillas
- Shredded cabbage or lettuce
- Diced tomatoes
- Sliced avocado
- Chopped cilantro
- Lime wedges, for serving
- Optional toppings: sour cream, salsa, hot sauce, etc.

Instructions:

1. In a large bowl, toss the shrimp with olive oil, chili powder, ground cumin, paprika, salt, and pepper until evenly coated.
2. Heat a large skillet or grill pan over medium-high heat. Add the seasoned shrimp to the skillet and cook for 2-3 minutes per side, or until they are pink and opaque.
3. Warm the tortillas in the skillet for about 30 seconds on each side, or until they are heated through and pliable.
4. To assemble the tacos, divide the cooked shrimp evenly among the tortillas.
5. Top each taco with shredded cabbage or lettuce, diced tomatoes, sliced avocado, and chopped cilantro.
6. Squeeze fresh lime juice over the tacos and serve with lime wedges on the side.
7. Serve the shrimp tacos immediately, with optional toppings such as sour cream, salsa, or hot sauce on the side.
8. Enjoy your delicious and flavorful shrimp tacos!

Feel free to customize your shrimp tacos with additional toppings such as diced onions, sliced jalapeños, or grated cheese. You can also use corn tortillas for a gluten-free option.

Veggie Omelette

Ingredients:

- 2-3 large eggs
- 1/4 cup diced vegetables (such as bell peppers, onions, tomatoes, spinach, mushrooms, etc.)
- 1 tablespoon olive oil or butter
- Salt and pepper, to taste
- Shredded cheese (optional)
- Fresh herbs (such as parsley, chives, or cilantro) for garnish (optional)

Instructions:

1. In a small bowl, beat the eggs together with a fork until well combined. Season with salt and pepper to taste.
2. Heat the olive oil or butter in a non-stick skillet over medium heat.
3. Add the diced vegetables to the skillet and sauté for 2-3 minutes, or until they are softened.
4. Pour the beaten eggs over the sautéed vegetables in the skillet, making sure to spread them out evenly.
5. Cook the omelette for 2-3 minutes, or until the edges start to set and the bottom is lightly golden brown.
6. If using cheese, sprinkle shredded cheese over one half of the omelette.
7. Using a spatula, carefully fold the other half of the omelette over the cheese (if using), creating a half-moon shape.
8. Cook the omelette for another 1-2 minutes, or until the cheese is melted and the eggs are cooked through.
9. Slide the veggie omelette onto a plate and garnish with fresh herbs, if desired.
10. Serve the veggie omelette hot, and enjoy your delicious and nutritious breakfast!

Feel free to customize your veggie omelette with your favorite vegetables and additional ingredients such as cooked ham, bacon, or sausage. You can also experiment with different cheese varieties to add extra flavor.

Turkey and Cheese Roll-Ups

Ingredients:

- Sliced turkey breast (deli-style)
- Sliced cheese (such as cheddar, Swiss, or provolone)
- Lettuce leaves
- Optional: mustard, mayonnaise, or other condiments
- Toothpicks or small skewers

Instructions:

1. Lay out a slice of turkey breast on a clean surface.
2. Place a slice of cheese on top of the turkey breast.
3. Add a lettuce leaf on top of the cheese.
4. If desired, spread a thin layer of mustard, mayonnaise, or other condiments over the lettuce leaf.
5. Starting at one end, tightly roll up the turkey breast, cheese, and lettuce into a cylinder shape.
6. Secure the roll-up with a toothpick or small skewer to hold it together.
7. Repeat the process with the remaining turkey breast slices, cheese, and lettuce.
8. Serve the turkey and cheese roll-ups immediately as a snack or light meal.

You can customize your turkey and cheese roll-ups by adding other ingredients such as sliced tomatoes, avocado, or bacon. Feel free to experiment with different condiments and cheese varieties to suit your taste preferences. Enjoy!

Spinach and Feta Stuffed Chicken Breast

Ingredients:

- 4 boneless, skinless chicken breasts
- 2 cups fresh spinach leaves, chopped
- 1/2 cup crumbled feta cheese
- 2 cloves garlic, minced
- 1 tablespoon olive oil
- Salt and pepper, to taste
- Toothpicks or kitchen twine, for securing the chicken

Instructions:

1. Preheat your oven to 375°F (190°C).
2. In a skillet, heat the olive oil over medium heat. Add the minced garlic and cook for 1-2 minutes, or until fragrant.
3. Add the chopped spinach to the skillet and cook until wilted, about 2-3 minutes. Remove from heat and let cool slightly.
4. In a mixing bowl, combine the cooked spinach with the crumbled feta cheese. Season with salt and pepper to taste.
5. Using a sharp knife, carefully slice a pocket into each chicken breast, being careful not to cut all the way through.
6. Stuff each chicken breast with the spinach and feta mixture, dividing it evenly among the chicken breasts.
7. Secure the openings of the chicken breasts with toothpicks or kitchen twine to prevent the stuffing from falling out.
8. Season the stuffed chicken breasts with salt and pepper on both sides.
9. Heat a skillet over medium-high heat. Add a drizzle of olive oil to the skillet.
10. Place the stuffed chicken breasts in the skillet and cook for 3-4 minutes on each side, or until golden brown.
11. Transfer the skillet to the preheated oven and bake for 15-20 minutes, or until the chicken is cooked through and reaches an internal temperature of 165°F (75°C).
12. Remove the stuffed chicken breasts from the oven and let them rest for a few minutes before serving.
13. Serve the spinach and feta stuffed chicken breasts hot, garnished with chopped parsley or a squeeze of lemon juice if desired.

Enjoy your delicious and flavorful stuffed chicken breasts!

Black Bean Quesadillas

Ingredients:

- 1 can (15 oz) black beans, drained and rinsed
- 1 cup shredded cheese (such as cheddar, Monterey Jack, or a Mexican blend)
- 1/2 cup salsa (store-bought or homemade)
- 1/4 cup chopped fresh cilantro
- 4 large flour tortillas
- Cooking oil or butter, for frying

Instructions:

1. In a mixing bowl, mash the black beans with a fork or potato masher until they are mostly smooth but still have some texture.
2. Stir in the shredded cheese, salsa, and chopped cilantro until well combined.
3. Lay out one flour tortilla on a clean surface. Spread a quarter of the black bean mixture evenly over half of the tortilla, leaving a small border around the edges.
4. Fold the other half of the tortilla over the filling to create a half-moon shape.
5. Repeat the process with the remaining tortillas and black bean mixture.
6. Heat a large skillet or frying pan over medium heat. Add a drizzle of cooking oil or a pat of butter to the skillet.
7. Carefully transfer one quesadilla to the skillet and cook for 2-3 minutes on each side, or until golden brown and crispy, and the cheese is melted.
8. Repeat the cooking process with the remaining quesadillas, adding more oil or butter to the skillet as needed.
9. Once cooked, remove the quesadillas from the skillet and let them cool for a minute before slicing into wedges.
10. Serve the black bean quesadillas hot, with optional toppings such as sour cream, guacamole, or additional salsa on the side.
11. Enjoy your delicious and flavorful black bean quesadillas as a snack, appetizer, or light meal!

Tuna Melt Sandwich

Ingredients:

- 2 cans (5 oz each) tuna, drained
- 1/4 cup mayonnaise
- 2 tablespoons finely chopped red onion
- 1 tablespoon chopped fresh parsley (optional)
- 1 tablespoon lemon juice
- Salt and pepper, to taste
- 4 slices of bread (such as white, whole wheat, or sourdough)
- 4 slices of cheese (such as cheddar, Swiss, or provolone)
- Butter or margarine, for spreading

Instructions:

1. In a mixing bowl, combine the drained tuna, mayonnaise, finely chopped red onion, chopped fresh parsley (if using), and lemon juice. Stir until well combined.
2. Season the tuna salad with salt and pepper to taste. Adjust seasoning if needed.
3. Preheat your oven's broiler or a panini press.
4. Spread butter or margarine on one side of each slice of bread.
5. Place the bread slices, buttered side down, on a baking sheet or preheated panini press.
6. Divide the tuna salad evenly among two slices of bread, spreading it out to cover the entire slice.
7. Place a slice of cheese on top of the tuna salad on each slice of bread.
8. Top each tuna melt with the remaining slices of bread, buttered side facing up.
9. If using a broiler, place the baking sheet under the broiler for 2-3 minutes, or until the cheese is melted and bubbly, and the bread is toasted.
10. If using a panini press, close the lid and cook the sandwiches for 3-4 minutes, or until the cheese is melted and the bread is toasted.
11. Remove the tuna melt sandwiches from the oven or panini press and let them cool for a minute before serving.
12. Slice the sandwiches in half diagonally, if desired, and serve hot.

Enjoy your delicious and cheesy tuna melt sandwiches!

Margherita Flatbread

Ingredients:

- 1 flatbread or pre-made pizza crust
- 1-2 ripe tomatoes, thinly sliced
- 1-2 cloves garlic, minced
- Fresh basil leaves
- 8 oz (225g) fresh mozzarella cheese, thinly sliced
- Olive oil
- Salt and pepper, to taste

Instructions:

1. Preheat your oven to the temperature recommended for your flatbread or pizza crust (usually around 400°F or 200°C).
2. Place the flatbread or pizza crust on a baking sheet lined with parchment paper.
3. Drizzle a little olive oil over the flatbread or pizza crust and spread it evenly with a pastry brush or the back of a spoon.
4. Sprinkle the minced garlic evenly over the oiled flatbread or pizza crust.
5. Arrange the thinly sliced tomatoes over the flatbread, covering the surface evenly.
6. Tear the fresh basil leaves into smaller pieces and scatter them over the tomatoes.
7. Place the thinly sliced fresh mozzarella cheese on top of the tomatoes and basil.
8. Drizzle a little more olive oil over the top of the flatbread.
9. Season with salt and pepper to taste.
10. Place the baking sheet in the preheated oven and bake for 10-15 minutes, or until the cheese is melted and bubbly and the edges of the flatbread are golden brown.
11. Remove the Margherita flatbread from the oven and let it cool for a minute or two before slicing.
12. Slice the flatbread into wedges or squares and serve hot.

Enjoy your delicious Margherita flatbread as an appetizer, snack, or light meal!

Chicken Fajitas

Ingredients:

- 1 lb (450g) boneless, skinless chicken breasts, sliced into thin strips
- 2 bell peppers (any color), thinly sliced
- 1 onion, thinly sliced
- 2 cloves garlic, minced
- 2 tablespoons olive oil
- 1 tablespoon chili powder
- 1 teaspoon ground cumin
- 1 teaspoon smoked paprika
- 1/2 teaspoon garlic powder
- 1/2 teaspoon onion powder
- Salt and pepper, to taste
- Flour tortillas, for serving
- Optional toppings: shredded cheese, sour cream, salsa, guacamole, chopped cilantro, lime wedges, etc.

Instructions:

1. In a small bowl, mix together the chili powder, ground cumin, smoked paprika, garlic powder, onion powder, salt, and pepper to create a fajita seasoning blend.
2. In a large skillet or frying pan, heat 1 tablespoon of olive oil over medium-high heat.
3. Add the sliced chicken to the skillet and sprinkle half of the fajita seasoning blend over the chicken. Cook, stirring occasionally, until the chicken is cooked through and no longer pink, about 5-7 minutes. Remove the chicken from the skillet and set aside.
4. In the same skillet, add the remaining tablespoon of olive oil. Add the sliced bell peppers, onion, and minced garlic to the skillet, and sprinkle the remaining fajita seasoning blend over the vegetables. Cook, stirring occasionally, until the vegetables are tender-crisp, about 5-7 minutes.
5. Return the cooked chicken to the skillet with the vegetables and toss everything together until well combined. Cook for an additional 2-3 minutes to heat the chicken through.
6. Warm the flour tortillas according to the package instructions.

7. To serve, spoon the chicken and vegetable mixture onto warm flour tortillas. Top with your favorite toppings such as shredded cheese, sour cream, salsa, guacamole, chopped cilantro, and a squeeze of lime juice.
8. Roll up the tortillas and enjoy your delicious chicken fajitas!

Feel free to customize your chicken fajitas with additional toppings and condiments to suit your taste preferences. You can also add sliced jalapeños or hot sauce for extra heat.

Pasta Primavera

Ingredients:

- 8 oz (225g) pasta (such as spaghetti, fettuccine, or penne)
- 2 tablespoons olive oil
- 2 cloves garlic, minced
- 1 onion, thinly sliced
- 2 carrots, julienned
- 1 bell pepper, thinly sliced
- 1 zucchini, julienned or sliced
- 1 yellow squash, julienned or sliced
- 1 cup cherry tomatoes, halved
- 1 cup broccoli florets
- 1/2 cup peas (fresh or frozen)
- Salt and pepper, to taste
- 1/4 cup grated Parmesan cheese (optional)
- Fresh basil or parsley, chopped, for garnish (optional)

Instructions:

1. Cook the pasta according to the package instructions until al dente. Drain and set aside.
2. In a large skillet or frying pan, heat the olive oil over medium heat. Add the minced garlic and sliced onion, and sauté until softened and fragrant, about 2-3 minutes.
3. Add the julienned carrots, sliced bell pepper, sliced zucchini, sliced yellow squash, halved cherry tomatoes, broccoli florets, and peas to the skillet. Season with salt and pepper to taste. Cook, stirring occasionally, until the vegetables are tender but still crisp, about 5-7 minutes.
4. Add the cooked pasta to the skillet with the vegetables. Toss everything together until well combined and heated through, about 2-3 minutes.
5. If desired, sprinkle grated Parmesan cheese over the pasta primavera and toss to combine.
6. Remove the skillet from heat and garnish with chopped fresh basil or parsley, if using.

7. Serve the pasta primavera hot, with additional grated Parmesan cheese on the side if desired.
8. Enjoy your delicious and colorful pasta primavera!

Feel free to customize your pasta primavera with your favorite spring vegetables and herbs. You can also add cooked chicken, shrimp, or tofu for extra protein if desired.

Cobb Salad

Ingredients:

- 4 cups chopped romaine lettuce
- 2 cups cooked chicken breast, diced or shredded
- 4 slices cooked bacon, crumbled
- 2 hard-boiled eggs, chopped
- 1 avocado, diced
- 1 cup cherry tomatoes, halved
- 1/2 cup crumbled blue cheese
- 1/4 cup chopped green onions or chives
- Salt and pepper, to taste
- Your favorite salad dressing (such as ranch, blue cheese, or balsamic vinaigrette)

Instructions:

1. In a large salad bowl, arrange the chopped romaine lettuce as the base of the salad.
2. Arrange the cooked chicken breast, crumbled bacon, chopped hard-boiled eggs, diced avocado, cherry tomatoes, and crumbled blue cheese in rows on top of the lettuce.
3. Sprinkle chopped green onions or chives over the salad.
4. Season the salad with salt and pepper to taste.
5. Drizzle your favorite salad dressing over the Cobb salad just before serving. You can use ranch dressing, blue cheese dressing, balsamic vinaigrette, or any other dressing you prefer.
6. Toss the salad gently to coat everything evenly with the dressing.
7. Serve the Cobb salad immediately, and enjoy!

Feel free to customize your Cobb salad with additional ingredients such as sliced cucumber, sliced bell peppers, black olives, or grilled corn. You can also add grilled chicken or steak for extra protein. Enjoy your delicious and satisfying Cobb salad!

Chicken Burrito Bowl

Ingredients:

- 1 cup cooked rice (white, brown, or Spanish rice)
- 1 cup cooked black beans (canned or homemade)
- 1 cup cooked corn kernels (fresh, canned, or frozen)
- 1 cup cooked chicken breast, diced or shredded
- 1 avocado, sliced
- 1/2 cup diced tomatoes
- 1/4 cup diced red onion
- 1/4 cup chopped fresh cilantro
- 1 lime, cut into wedges
- Salt and pepper, to taste
- Optional toppings: shredded cheese, sour cream, salsa, guacamole, chopped lettuce, sliced jalapeños, etc.

Instructions:

1. Cook the rice according to the package instructions. Fluff with a fork and set aside.
2. In a medium saucepan, heat the black beans and corn kernels over medium heat until warmed through. Season with salt and pepper to taste.
3. Cook the chicken breast in a skillet over medium heat until cooked through and no longer pink in the center. Season with salt and pepper to taste. Once cooked, dice or shred the chicken.
4. Assemble the burrito bowls: Divide the cooked rice among serving bowls. Top each bowl with a portion of the cooked black beans, corn kernels, and chicken breast.
5. Add the sliced avocado, diced tomatoes, diced red onion, and chopped fresh cilantro to each bowl.
6. Squeeze fresh lime juice over the burrito bowls and season with additional salt and pepper to taste.
7. If desired, add optional toppings such as shredded cheese, sour cream, salsa, guacamole, chopped lettuce, sliced jalapeños, etc.
8. Serve the chicken burrito bowls immediately, and enjoy!

Feel free to customize your chicken burrito bowls with your favorite ingredients and toppings. You can also add cooked bell peppers, onions, or other vegetables for extra flavor and nutrients. Enjoy your delicious and satisfying meal!

Ratatouille

Ingredients:

- 1 large eggplant, diced
- 2 zucchinis, diced
- 1 yellow squash, diced
- 1 onion, diced
- 2 bell peppers (red, yellow, or green), diced
- 4 cloves garlic, minced
- 4 tomatoes, diced (or 1 can diced tomatoes)
- 2 tablespoons tomato paste
- 2 tablespoons olive oil
- 1 teaspoon dried thyme
- 1 teaspoon dried oregano
- Salt and pepper, to taste
- Fresh basil or parsley, chopped, for garnish (optional)

Instructions:

1. Heat the olive oil in a large skillet or Dutch oven over medium heat.
2. Add the diced onion and minced garlic to the skillet and sauté until softened and fragrant, about 3-4 minutes.
3. Add the diced eggplant, zucchini, yellow squash, and bell peppers to the skillet. Cook, stirring occasionally, until the vegetables are slightly softened, about 5-6 minutes.
4. Stir in the diced tomatoes, tomato paste, dried thyme, dried oregano, salt, and pepper. Mix until well combined.
5. Reduce the heat to low, cover the skillet, and simmer the ratatouille for about 20-25 minutes, stirring occasionally, until the vegetables are tender and the flavors have melded together.
6. Taste and adjust the seasoning with salt and pepper, if needed.
7. Once cooked, remove the skillet from heat and let the ratatouille cool slightly.
8. Serve the ratatouille hot or at room temperature, garnished with chopped fresh basil or parsley if desired.

Ratatouille can be served as a main dish with crusty bread or cooked grains such as rice or quinoa, or as a side dish alongside grilled meats or fish. Enjoy this delicious and flavorful French vegetable stew!

Egg and Avocado Breakfast Wrap

Ingredients:

- 1 large egg
- 1 large whole wheat or flour tortilla
- 1/2 ripe avocado, sliced or mashed
- Handful of baby spinach leaves
- Salt and pepper, to taste
- Optional toppings: shredded cheese, salsa, hot sauce, diced tomatoes, chopped cilantro, etc.

Instructions:

1. Heat a non-stick skillet over medium heat. Crack the egg into the skillet and cook until the white is set and the yolk is cooked to your desired level of doneness (such as over easy, over medium, or scrambled).
2. While the egg is cooking, warm the tortilla in a separate skillet or in the microwave for a few seconds until it's soft and pliable.
3. Once the egg is cooked, remove it from the skillet and set it aside.
4. Spread the mashed avocado onto the center of the tortilla, leaving a border around the edges.
5. Place the cooked egg on top of the mashed avocado.
6. Add a handful of baby spinach leaves on top of the egg.
7. Season with salt and pepper to taste.
8. If desired, add optional toppings such as shredded cheese, salsa, hot sauce, diced tomatoes, or chopped cilantro on top of the spinach.
9. Fold the sides of the tortilla over the filling, then roll it up tightly into a wrap.
10. Cut the wrap in half diagonally, if desired, and serve immediately.

Enjoy your delicious and nutritious egg and avocado breakfast wrap! You can customize it with your favorite toppings and add-ins to suit your taste preferences.

Buffalo Chicken Wraps

Ingredients:

- 2 boneless, skinless chicken breasts
- 1/4 cup buffalo sauce
- 2 tablespoons ranch or blue cheese dressing
- 4 large flour tortillas
- 1 cup shredded lettuce
- 1/2 cup diced tomatoes
- 1/4 cup diced red onion
- 1/4 cup crumbled blue cheese (optional)
- Salt and pepper, to taste
- Cooking oil or cooking spray, for cooking the chicken

Instructions:

1. Season the chicken breasts with salt and pepper on both sides.
2. Heat a skillet or grill pan over medium-high heat and lightly grease it with cooking oil or cooking spray.
3. Cook the chicken breasts for 5-6 minutes on each side, or until they are cooked through and no longer pink in the center.
4. Remove the cooked chicken from the skillet and let it rest for a few minutes.
5. Once the chicken has cooled slightly, slice it into thin strips.
6. In a small bowl, mix together the buffalo sauce and ranch or blue cheese dressing until well combined.
7. Lay out the flour tortillas on a clean surface.
8. Divide the shredded lettuce evenly among the tortillas, spreading it out in the center of each tortilla.
9. Top the lettuce with the sliced chicken strips.
10. Drizzle the buffalo sauce mixture over the chicken.
11. Sprinkle diced tomatoes, diced red onion, and crumbled blue cheese (if using) over the chicken.
12. Fold the sides of the tortillas over the filling, then roll them up tightly into wraps.
13. Cut the wraps in half diagonally, if desired, and serve immediately.

Enjoy your delicious buffalo chicken wraps! You can customize them with additional toppings such as sliced avocado, chopped cilantro, or extra buffalo sauce for added flavor.

Quinoa Salad with Veggies

Ingredients:

- 1 cup quinoa, rinsed
- 2 cups water or vegetable broth
- 1 red bell pepper, diced
- 1 yellow bell pepper, diced
- 1 cucumber, diced
- 1 cup cherry tomatoes, halved
- 1/4 cup red onion, finely chopped
- 1/4 cup fresh parsley, chopped
- 1/4 cup fresh basil, chopped
- 1/4 cup feta cheese, crumbled (optional)
- 1/4 cup sliced almonds or pine nuts (optional)
- Salt and pepper, to taste

For the dressing:

- 1/4 cup extra virgin olive oil
- 2 tablespoons lemon juice or white wine vinegar
- 1 garlic clove, minced
- 1 teaspoon Dijon mustard
- 1 teaspoon honey or maple syrup
- Salt and pepper, to taste

Instructions:

1. In a medium saucepan, combine the quinoa and water or vegetable broth. Bring to a boil, then reduce the heat to low, cover, and simmer for 15-20 minutes, or until the quinoa is cooked and the liquid is absorbed. Remove from heat and let it cool.
2. In a large mixing bowl, combine the cooked quinoa with the diced red and yellow bell peppers, diced cucumber, halved cherry tomatoes, chopped red onion, chopped parsley, and chopped basil. Toss to combine.

3. In a small bowl, whisk together the extra virgin olive oil, lemon juice or white wine vinegar, minced garlic, Dijon mustard, honey or maple syrup, salt, and pepper to make the dressing.
4. Pour the dressing over the quinoa and vegetable mixture, and toss until everything is well coated.
5. If using, sprinkle crumbled feta cheese and sliced almonds or pine nuts over the salad.
6. Season with additional salt and pepper, if needed.
7. Cover the salad and refrigerate for at least 30 minutes to allow the flavors to meld together.
8. Before serving, give the salad a final toss and adjust the seasoning if needed.
9. Serve the quinoa salad with veggies chilled or at room temperature.

Enjoy your delicious and nutritious quinoa salad with veggies! It's perfect as a side dish or a light meal on its own.

Grilled Chicken Caesar Wrap

Ingredients:

- 2 boneless, skinless chicken breasts
- Salt and pepper, to taste
- 4 large flour tortillas
- 2 cups chopped romaine lettuce
- 1/4 cup grated Parmesan cheese
- Caesar salad dressing (store-bought or homemade)
- Optional: croutons, for added crunch

Instructions:

1. Preheat a grill or grill pan over medium-high heat.
2. Season the chicken breasts with salt and pepper on both sides.
3. Place the seasoned chicken breasts on the preheated grill and cook for 6-8 minutes on each side, or until they are cooked through and no longer pink in the center. Remove from the grill and let them rest for a few minutes.
4. Once the chicken has rested, slice it into thin strips.
5. Warm the flour tortillas in a skillet or microwave for a few seconds until they are soft and pliable.
6. To assemble the wraps, lay out the flour tortillas on a clean surface.
7. Divide the chopped romaine lettuce evenly among the tortillas, spreading it out in the center of each tortilla.
8. Top the lettuce with the sliced grilled chicken strips.
9. Sprinkle grated Parmesan cheese over the chicken.
10. Drizzle Caesar salad dressing over the chicken and cheese.
11. Add croutons, if using, for added crunch.
12. Fold the sides of the tortillas over the filling, then roll them up tightly into wraps.
13. Cut the wraps in half diagonally, if desired, and serve immediately.

Enjoy your delicious grilled chicken Caesar wraps! They're packed with flavor and make for a satisfying meal option.

Turkey Chili

Ingredients:

- 1 tablespoon olive oil
- 1 onion, diced
- 2 cloves garlic, minced
- 1 bell pepper, diced (any color)
- 1 pound ground turkey
- 1 can (14.5 oz) diced tomatoes
- 1 can (15 oz) tomato sauce
- 1 can (15 oz) kidney beans, drained and rinsed
- 1 can (15 oz) black beans, drained and rinsed
- 1 cup corn kernels (fresh, canned, or frozen)
- 2 tablespoons chili powder
- 1 teaspoon ground cumin
- 1 teaspoon paprika
- Salt and pepper, to taste
- Optional toppings: shredded cheese, sour cream, chopped green onions, chopped cilantro, diced avocado, etc.

Instructions:

1. Heat the olive oil in a large pot or Dutch oven over medium heat.
2. Add the diced onion, minced garlic, and diced bell pepper to the pot. Cook, stirring occasionally, until the vegetables are softened, about 5-6 minutes.
3. Add the ground turkey to the pot, breaking it up with a spoon. Cook until the turkey is browned and cooked through, about 6-7 minutes.
4. Stir in the diced tomatoes, tomato sauce, kidney beans, black beans, corn kernels, chili powder, ground cumin, paprika, salt, and pepper.
5. Bring the chili to a simmer, then reduce the heat to low. Cover and let the chili simmer for about 20-30 minutes, stirring occasionally, to allow the flavors to meld together.
6. Taste and adjust the seasoning with salt and pepper, if needed.
7. Once the chili is cooked and heated through, remove it from the heat.
8. Serve the turkey chili hot, garnished with your favorite toppings such as shredded cheese, sour cream, chopped green onions, chopped cilantro, diced avocado, etc.

9. Enjoy your delicious and comforting turkey chili!

Turkey chili is versatile and can be customized to suit your taste preferences. Feel free to adjust the seasonings and add extra ingredients such as diced tomatoes, bell peppers, or jalapeños for extra flavor and heat.

Veggie Stir-Fry with Tofu

Ingredients:

- 14 oz (400g) extra firm tofu, pressed and cut into cubes
- 2 tablespoons soy sauce or tamari
- 1 tablespoon cornstarch
- 2 tablespoons vegetable oil, divided
- 2 cloves garlic, minced
- 1 tablespoon minced ginger
- 1 onion, sliced
- 2 bell peppers (any color), sliced
- 1 carrot, julienned or sliced into thin strips
- 1 cup broccoli florets
- 1 cup snow peas or snap peas
- 1 cup sliced mushrooms (such as shiitake or button mushrooms)
- 2 tablespoons hoisin sauce
- 1 tablespoon rice vinegar
- Cooked rice or noodles, for serving

Instructions:

1. In a bowl, combine the cubed tofu with soy sauce (or tamari) and cornstarch. Toss gently to coat the tofu evenly.
2. Heat 1 tablespoon of vegetable oil in a large skillet or wok over medium-high heat. Add the tofu cubes and cook until they are golden brown and crispy on all sides, about 5-7 minutes. Remove the tofu from the skillet and set aside.
3. In the same skillet, add the remaining tablespoon of vegetable oil. Add the minced garlic and minced ginger, and sauté for about 30 seconds, until fragrant.
4. Add the sliced onion, bell peppers, julienned carrot, broccoli florets, snow peas, and sliced mushrooms to the skillet. Stir-fry for 5-6 minutes, or until the vegetables are tender-crisp.
5. Return the cooked tofu to the skillet with the vegetables.
6. In a small bowl, mix together the hoisin sauce and rice vinegar. Pour the sauce over the tofu and vegetables in the skillet. Stir to coat everything evenly.
7. Cook for an additional 2-3 minutes, stirring occasionally, until the sauce has thickened slightly and everything is heated through.

8. Remove the skillet from heat.
9. Serve the veggie stir-fry with tofu hot, over cooked rice or noodles.

Enjoy your delicious and flavorful veggie stir-fry with tofu! You can customize it with your favorite vegetables and adjust the seasonings to suit your taste preferences.

Chicken and Rice Soup

Ingredients:

- 1 tablespoon olive oil
- 1 onion, diced
- 2 carrots, diced
- 2 celery stalks, diced
- 2 cloves garlic, minced
- 6 cups chicken broth
- 1 cup cooked chicken breast, shredded or diced
- 1 cup cooked white rice
- Salt and pepper, to taste
- Fresh parsley, chopped, for garnish (optional)

Instructions:

1. Heat the olive oil in a large pot over medium heat. Add the diced onion, carrots, and celery, and sauté until the vegetables are softened, about 5-6 minutes.
2. Add the minced garlic to the pot and sauté for an additional 1-2 minutes, until fragrant.
3. Pour the chicken broth into the pot and bring it to a simmer.
4. Once the broth is simmering, add the cooked chicken breast and cooked white rice to the pot. Stir to combine.
5. Season the soup with salt and pepper to taste. Keep in mind that the chicken broth may already be seasoned, so adjust the seasoning accordingly.
6. Let the soup simmer for 10-15 minutes to allow the flavors to meld together and the chicken and rice to heat through.
7. Taste the soup and adjust the seasoning with more salt and pepper, if needed.
8. Once the soup is heated through and seasoned to your liking, remove it from the heat.
9. Ladle the chicken and rice soup into bowls and garnish with chopped fresh parsley, if desired.
10. Serve the soup hot and enjoy!

Feel free to customize your chicken and rice soup by adding other vegetables such as peas, corn, or spinach. You can also add herbs and spices like thyme or rosemary for extra flavor.

Beef Tacos

Ingredients:

- 1 lb (450g) ground beef
- 1 tablespoon olive oil (if needed)
- 1 onion, diced
- 2 cloves garlic, minced
- 1 tablespoon chili powder
- 1 teaspoon ground cumin
- 1/2 teaspoon paprika
- 1/4 teaspoon dried oregano
- Salt and pepper, to taste
- 1/2 cup tomato sauce
- 1/4 cup water
- 8 small corn or flour tortillas
- Optional toppings: shredded lettuce, diced tomatoes, shredded cheese, diced avocado, sour cream, salsa, chopped cilantro, lime wedges, etc.

Instructions:

1. Heat a large skillet over medium-high heat. If using lean ground beef, you may need to add a tablespoon of olive oil to the skillet.
2. Add the diced onion to the skillet and cook until softened, about 3-4 minutes.
3. Add the minced garlic to the skillet and cook for an additional 1-2 minutes, until fragrant.
4. Add the ground beef to the skillet, breaking it up with a spoon. Cook until the beef is browned and cooked through, about 6-7 minutes.
5. Once the beef is cooked, drain any excess fat from the skillet.
6. Stir in the chili powder, ground cumin, paprika, dried oregano, salt, and pepper. Cook for 1-2 minutes, until the spices are fragrant.
7. Add the tomato sauce and water to the skillet, stirring to combine. Reduce the heat to low and simmer the beef mixture for 5-10 minutes, until thickened.
8. While the beef mixture is simmering, warm the tortillas in a skillet or microwave until they are soft and pliable.
9. To assemble the tacos, spoon some of the beef mixture onto each tortilla. Add your desired toppings such as shredded lettuce, diced tomatoes, shredded

    cheese, diced avocado, sour cream, salsa, chopped cilantro, and a squeeze of lime juice.
11. Serve the beef tacos immediately, and enjoy!

Feel free to customize your beef tacos with your favorite toppings and add-ins. You can also use hard taco shells instead of soft tortillas if you prefer.

Avocado and Tomato Grilled Cheese

Ingredients:

- 4 slices of bread (any type you prefer)
- 1 ripe avocado, thinly sliced
- 1 large tomato, thinly sliced
- 1 cup shredded cheese (cheddar, mozzarella, or any cheese you like)
- Butter or margarine, softened

Instructions:

1. Heat a skillet or griddle over medium heat.
2. Butter one side of each slice of bread.
3. Place two slices of bread, buttered side down, on the skillet or griddle.
4. Layer the avocado slices, tomato slices, and shredded cheese evenly on top of the bread slices.
5. Place the remaining slices of bread on top, buttered side facing up.
6. Cook the sandwiches for 3-4 minutes on each side, or until the bread is golden brown and the cheese is melted.
7. Once cooked, remove the sandwiches from the skillet or griddle and let them cool for a minute.
8. Cut the sandwiches in half diagonally, if desired, and serve hot.

Enjoy your delicious avocado and tomato grilled cheese sandwiches! They're perfect for a quick and satisfying meal. Feel free to customize them with additional ingredients like bacon, spinach, or sliced turkey for extra flavor.

Greek Yogurt Chicken Salad

Ingredients:

- 2 cups cooked chicken breast, shredded or diced
- 1/2 cup Greek yogurt (plain or flavored)
- 1/4 cup diced celery
- 1/4 cup diced red onion
- 1/4 cup diced apple
- 1/4 cup sliced grapes
- 2 tablespoons chopped pecans or walnuts (optional)
- 1 tablespoon lemon juice
- 1 teaspoon Dijon mustard
- Salt and pepper, to taste
- Fresh parsley or dill, chopped, for garnish (optional)

Instructions:

1. In a large mixing bowl, combine the shredded or diced chicken breast, Greek yogurt, diced celery, diced red onion, diced apple, sliced grapes, and chopped pecans or walnuts (if using).
2. Add the lemon juice and Dijon mustard to the bowl. Stir everything together until well combined.
3. Season the chicken salad with salt and pepper to taste. Adjust the seasoning according to your preference.
4. Cover the bowl and refrigerate the chicken salad for at least 30 minutes to allow the flavors to meld together.
5. Once chilled, give the chicken salad a final stir.
6. Garnish the chicken salad with chopped fresh parsley or dill, if desired, before serving.
7. Serve the Greek yogurt chicken salad chilled, on its own, or in sandwiches, wraps, or lettuce cups.

Enjoy your delicious and nutritious Greek yogurt chicken salad! It's perfect for a light lunch, snack, or meal prep. Feel free to customize it with your favorite add-ins such as dried cranberries, chopped almonds, or diced avocado.

Lentil Soup

Ingredients:

- 1 tablespoon olive oil
- 1 onion, diced
- 2 carrots, diced
- 2 celery stalks, diced
- 2 cloves garlic, minced
- 1 cup dried lentils (green or brown), rinsed and drained
- 4 cups vegetable broth or chicken broth
- 1 can (14.5 oz) diced tomatoes
- 1 teaspoon ground cumin
- 1 teaspoon ground coriander
- 1/2 teaspoon smoked paprika
- 1/4 teaspoon cayenne pepper (optional, for heat)
- Salt and pepper, to taste
- Fresh parsley or cilantro, chopped, for garnish (optional)
- Lemon wedges, for serving (optional)

Instructions:

1. Heat the olive oil in a large pot over medium heat. Add the diced onion, carrots, and celery, and sauté until the vegetables are softened, about 5-6 minutes.
2. Add the minced garlic to the pot and sauté for an additional 1-2 minutes, until fragrant.
3. Add the dried lentils, vegetable broth or chicken broth, diced tomatoes (with their juices), ground cumin, ground coriander, smoked paprika, and cayenne pepper (if using) to the pot. Stir to combine.
4. Bring the soup to a boil, then reduce the heat to low and simmer, covered, for 25-30 minutes, or until the lentils are tender.
5. Once the lentils are cooked, taste the soup and season with salt and pepper to taste. Adjust the seasoning according to your preference.
6. If you prefer a smoother soup, you can use an immersion blender to blend part of the soup until it reaches your desired consistency. Alternatively, you can leave the soup as is for a chunkier texture.

7. Serve the lentil soup hot, garnished with chopped fresh parsley or cilantro, if desired. Serve with lemon wedges on the side for squeezing over the soup, if desired.
8. Enjoy your delicious and comforting lentil soup!

Lentil soup is versatile and can be customized with your favorite vegetables and spices. Feel free to add chopped spinach, kale, or other leafy greens for extra nutrition. You can also add diced potatoes or sweet potatoes for a heartier soup.

Beef Stir-Fry with Broccoli

Ingredients:

- 1 lb (450g) beef sirloin or flank steak, thinly sliced against the grain
- 2 tablespoons soy sauce
- 1 tablespoon oyster sauce
- 1 tablespoon cornstarch
- 2 tablespoons vegetable oil, divided
- 2 cloves garlic, minced
- 1 teaspoon minced ginger
- 1 head broccoli, cut into florets
- 1 bell pepper, sliced (any color)
- 1 onion, sliced
- Salt and pepper, to taste
- Cooked rice or noodles, for serving

Instructions:

1. In a bowl, combine the thinly sliced beef with soy sauce, oyster sauce, and cornstarch. Toss to coat the beef evenly and set aside to marinate for at least 15 minutes.
2. Heat 1 tablespoon of vegetable oil in a large skillet or wok over medium-high heat. Add the minced garlic and minced ginger to the skillet and sauté for about 30 seconds, until fragrant.
3. Add the marinated beef to the skillet and stir-fry for 2-3 minutes, or until the beef is browned and cooked through. Remove the beef from the skillet and set aside.
4. In the same skillet, add the remaining tablespoon of vegetable oil. Add the broccoli florets, sliced bell pepper, and sliced onion to the skillet. Stir-fry for 3-4 minutes, or until the vegetables are tender-crisp.
5. Return the cooked beef to the skillet with the vegetables. Stir to combine everything evenly.
6. Season the stir-fry with salt and pepper to taste. Adjust the seasoning according to your preference.
7. Cook for an additional 1-2 minutes, stirring constantly, until everything is heated through.
8. Once cooked, remove the skillet from heat.
9. Serve the beef stir-fry with broccoli hot, over cooked rice or noodles.

Enjoy your delicious and flavorful beef stir-fry with broccoli! It's perfect for a quick and satisfying meal. Feel free to customize it with your favorite vegetables and add-ins.

Spinach and Mushroom Quesadillas

Ingredients:

- 4 large flour tortillas
- 2 cups fresh spinach leaves
- 1 cup sliced mushrooms (button or cremini)
- 1/2 cup diced onion
- 1 clove garlic, minced
- 1 cup shredded cheese (cheddar, mozzarella, or a blend)
- 2 tablespoons olive oil or butter, divided
- Salt and pepper, to taste
- Optional toppings: salsa, sour cream, guacamole, chopped cilantro, etc.

Instructions:

1. Heat 1 tablespoon of olive oil or butter in a skillet over medium heat. Add the diced onion and sliced mushrooms to the skillet and sauté until the vegetables are softened, about 5-6 minutes.
2. Add the minced garlic to the skillet and sauté for an additional 1-2 minutes, until fragrant.
3. Add the fresh spinach leaves to the skillet and cook until wilted, about 2-3 minutes. Season with salt and pepper to taste. Remove the skillet from heat and set aside.
4. Place a large skillet or griddle over medium heat. Brush one side of each flour tortilla with a little olive oil or butter.
5. Place one tortilla, oiled side down, in the skillet. Sprinkle a layer of shredded cheese over the tortilla, followed by a layer of the spinach and mushroom mixture.
6. Place another tortilla on top, oiled side up.
7. Cook the quesadilla for 2-3 minutes on each side, or until the tortillas are golden brown and the cheese is melted.
8. Remove the quesadilla from the skillet and let it cool for a minute before slicing into wedges.
9. Repeat the process with the remaining tortillas and filling ingredients.
10. Serve the spinach and mushroom quesadillas hot, with optional toppings such as salsa, sour cream, guacamole, or chopped cilantro on the side.

Enjoy your delicious spinach and mushroom quesadillas! They make for a satisfying meal or snack that's packed with flavor and nutrients. Feel free to customize them with your favorite cheeses or additional fillings like black beans or diced peppers.

Shrimp Stir-Fry with Rice

Ingredients:

- 1 lb (450g) medium shrimp, peeled and deveined
- 2 cups cooked rice (white or brown)
- 2 tablespoons soy sauce
- 1 tablespoon oyster sauce
- 1 tablespoon sesame oil
- 1 tablespoon vegetable oil
- 2 cloves garlic, minced
- 1 teaspoon minced ginger
- 1 bell pepper, sliced (any color)
- 1 cup broccoli florets
- 1 carrot, julienned or sliced into thin strips
- 1/2 cup sliced mushrooms (such as shiitake or button mushrooms)
- Salt and pepper, to taste
- Optional garnish: chopped green onions, sesame seeds

Instructions:

1. In a bowl, combine the shrimp with soy sauce, oyster sauce, and sesame oil. Toss to coat the shrimp evenly and set aside to marinate for at least 15 minutes.
2. Heat vegetable oil in a large skillet or wok over medium-high heat. Add minced garlic and minced ginger to the skillet and sauté for about 30 seconds, until fragrant.
3. Add the marinated shrimp to the skillet and stir-fry for 2-3 minutes, or until the shrimp turn pink and opaque. Remove the shrimp from the skillet and set aside.
4. In the same skillet, add sliced bell pepper, broccoli florets, julienned carrot, and sliced mushrooms. Stir-fry for 3-4 minutes, or until the vegetables are tender-crisp.
5. Return the cooked shrimp to the skillet with the vegetables. Stir to combine everything evenly.
6. Add the cooked rice to the skillet and stir-fry for an additional 2-3 minutes, or until the rice is heated through and well combined with the shrimp and vegetables.
7. Season the stir-fry with salt and pepper to taste. Adjust the seasoning according to your preference.
8. Once cooked, remove the skillet from heat.

9. Serve the shrimp stir-fry with rice hot, garnished with chopped green onions and sesame seeds, if desired.

Enjoy your delicious and flavorful shrimp stir-fry with rice! It's perfect for a quick and easy weeknight meal. Feel free to customize it with your favorite vegetables and add-ins.

Caprese Panini

Ingredients:

- 4 slices of ciabatta bread (or any other crusty bread)
- 2 ripe tomatoes, thinly sliced
- 8 ounces (225g) fresh mozzarella cheese, thinly sliced
- Fresh basil leaves
- Balsamic glaze (store-bought or homemade)
- Olive oil, for brushing

Instructions:

1. Preheat a panini press or grill pan over medium heat.
2. Brush one side of each slice of bread lightly with olive oil.
3. Place the bread slices, oiled side down, on a clean surface.
4. Layer the mozzarella cheese slices, tomato slices, and fresh basil leaves on two of the bread slices.
5. Drizzle a little balsamic glaze over the filling.
6. Place the remaining bread slices on top to form sandwiches, with the oiled side facing up.
7. Place the sandwiches on the preheated panini press or grill pan.
8. Cook the sandwiches for 3-4 minutes, or until the bread is golden brown and the cheese is melted.
9. Once cooked, remove the sandwiches from the panini press or grill pan.
10. Cut the sandwiches in half diagonally, if desired, and serve hot.

Enjoy your delicious Caprese panini! Serve it as a light lunch or dinner, accompanied by a side salad or some potato chips.

www.ingramcontent.com/pod-product-compliance
Lightning Source LLC
LaVergne TN
LVHW081619060526
838201LV00054B/2319